Seeds of Truth

IS

More **Seeds of Truth**

by Petra Eiko:

> Fear
> Sex
> Power
> Heart
> Sound
> Vision
> Wisdom

Seeds of Truth

IS

Petra Eiko

Red Hen Press Los Angeles 2001

Is
Copyright © 2001 by Petra Eiko

All Rights Reserved

No part of this book may be used or reproduced in any manner whatever without the prior written permission except in the case of brief quotations embodied in critical articles and reviews. Printed in Canada

Book and cover design by Mark E. Cull

ISBN 1-888996-38-2

First Edition

Red Hen Press
www.redhen.org

Thank you very much
Helmut, Rachel, Momo, Kate and Mark
for your trust, support and effort to bring this book into existence.

For my father *Heinz*!

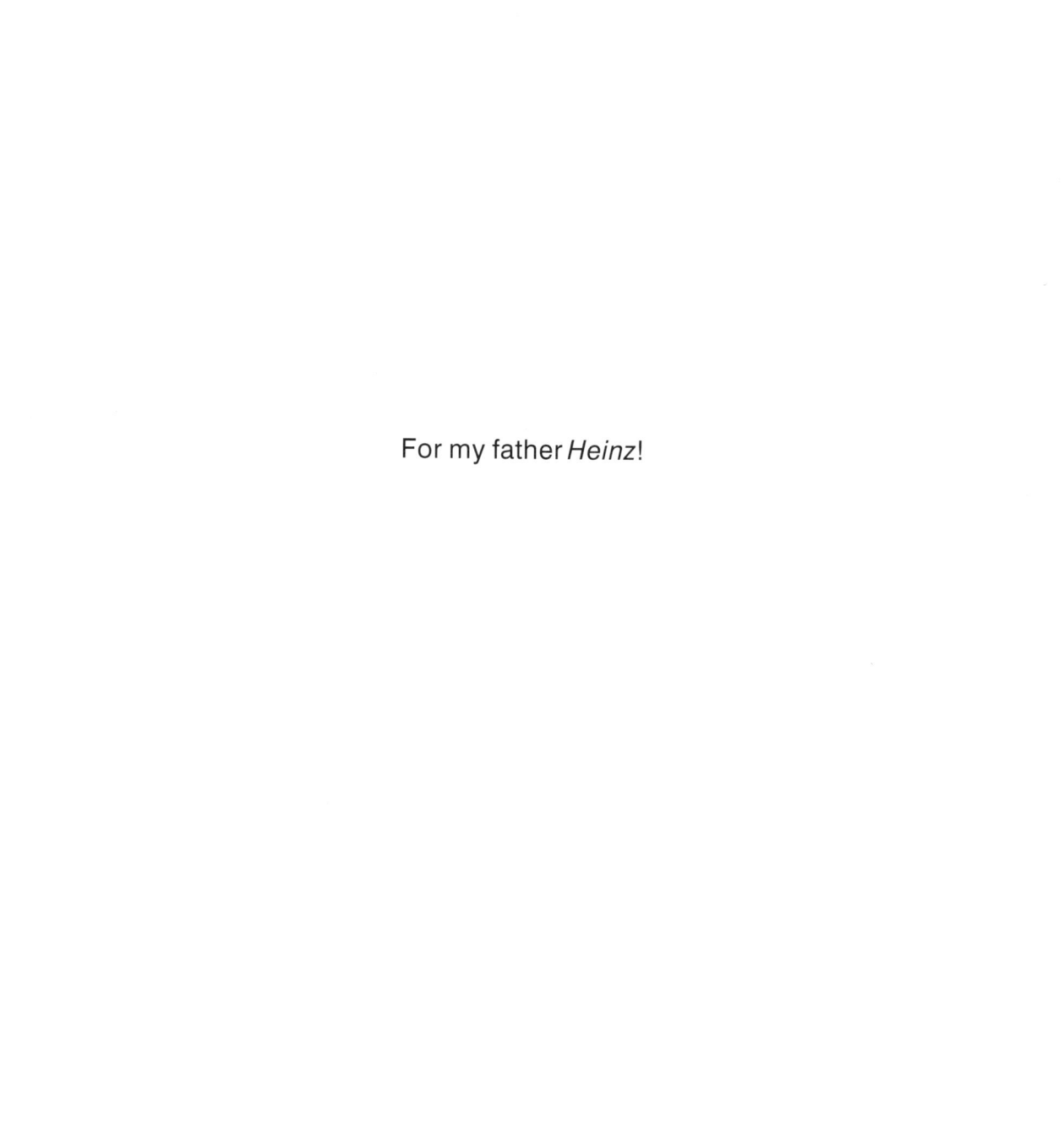

Hello dear Friend, I am "Is!"

Do you have any questions you'd like to ask me?

Who are you?

I am that of which you have no idea "what you are talking about" if you are talking about me!

Dear friend, let me introduce myself to you . . .

I
I am
I am "IS."
I am "IS" from where everything rises.
I am the emptiness from where the first breath emerged, to create the first thought.
I am the essence within the essence.
I am the beginning of all beginnings.
I am the creator of the creation.
I am the silence before matter.
I am everything and nothing.
I am the simplicity in itself.
I am the complete.
I am just "IS."
I am
I

I am that, for which you have no words.
I am "IS" and as by now, only a few of you got a glimpse of me.

That's who I am!

Do you have a body?

Well, yes and no! It will be a little difficult for you to understand, I know, but I "am" body and I am "no" body.

Or let me start this way:
What form of body would you like me to have. . . ? A body like yours? I can take on any form or body you can think of. Therefore I can slip into a body that looks exactly like yours. But think about it . . . why should I use a body like this?

I am moving between universes in an instant. This makes the speed of light much slower than "slow motion!" Why should I drag a body like yours around? It is fragile, needs constant care and nourishment. Look what happens with the bodies of your astronauts, when they make their tiny little trips into space. Among a lot of other problems their muscular consistency shrinks.

Can you imagine what would happen to your kind of body, if I would move it, with the speed I travel? After a couple of miles, there would be only a skeleton flying through space. . . ! and soon after that, the first bone would fly away!

No, no . . . it would only slow me down. Your body is created for the particular life on this particular planet "earth!"

My mobility is limitless. Therefore, I do not use a body like yours.

Okay, but then what do you look like?

I am coming to that in a minute, but before, let me tell you that you are talking out of your perspective. You'd like to see me in a "form," to "know" that I am existing, right?

See, what makes you confused is the fact, that in your concept of living, you always need "proof of existence." It is very hard for you to visualize something that you can not physically see. So, if I take on the shape of mankind and appear in front of you, shake your hand, sit and talk to you at your dinner table, show you some miracles and then disappear into nothing, I would have proven my existence to you.

You probably would shake like an earthquake for the next three days, but all of a sudden you would be convinced that I exist!

Even if I did that, it wouldn't be of any help to you. You would tell your friends and they would reduce your true story simply into a story of "fiction." After a while you would persuade yourself, that it was only a dream you had. It couldn't possibly be "reality!" Or you would start asking me to appear before your friends and perform some miracles. This would verify your story and also prove my existence to them . . . but then what?

After a while they would ask me for the same performance, to confirm their report to others, and so on!

You will agree, that this would be a **very poor occupation** for me!

You accept the world of macrocosm, microcosm and nanocosm, because your scientists and chemists succeeded to make this visible and therefore understandable for you. Now you are learning about "Neutrinos" because you have an image of them. You always need certain evidence to acknowledge an existence . . . any kind of existence, whatever it may be!

This is the way the teachings on earth have been for hundreds of years.

Please do not blame this on me, because the living concept you've lived in for the past hundreds of years, mankind created. This results out of your own creating powers. You created the thought that everything has to be proven by feel, thought, taste, hearing, visualizing or through measuring by certified machinery, to be "reality." Then it is "known" and in "existence!"

If you can not provide at least one kind of proof from the above, you identify this matter as "Believing." This classification is totally different from "Reality" and not to be taken too seriously. You call it absurd, or a lot of nonsense, mumbo jumbo or even baloney, because:
"Who knows if it exists, if it is true or real? Nobody knows!"

You have only one big exception in this systematization . . . this is "Religion." Religion is based on "Believing," because nobody can provide **anyone,** with any kind of "proof." Since most of you agreed a long time ago that "Religion" is serious business you decided it should be in the category "reality." But here you run into a conflict with your theory of proven "reality."

There is no proof to put religion into the category "Reality."

At that time, you did not see a different answer to your problem, but to enforce religion to get it into your self-created vision of "reality." The "quick fix" for your conflict was, to base "Religion" on "Fear." Poor fear . . . for a long time, it was quite abused to fit your evasive solution to your troubles!

But, I am getting sidetracked here, let me come back to your question. What was it again?

Don't worry, I know it exactly. You still have no idea what I look like!

Let me see . . . how can I explain this to you, with your known words? Stay with me, maybe I can clarify it for you!

My body consists of pure concentrated energy. It is "all" energy in existence, filtered down into "absolute purity." It is beyond energy like you know it, on your planet earth. It is so much denser and so much more powerful. Just think about it: . . . I am holding all energy of all universes and all spaces in my body!

That's quite a bit of energy . . . don't you agree?

If you could see me with your eyes, you would observe me as the brightest light you have ever seen. This is what I look like, this is my body!

This light is my energy, which is so immensely condensed it is "silent." It is in total balance, the peace within the peace. At first sight my light would appear to you to be standing still . . . without any movement.

But without any doubt, there is movement in me . . . **and plenty!** You will experience it, if you would look a bit more closely!

I am *"the"* light, the ultimate light, wherein everything *"is."* In my light everything is melted together into the complete. All wisdom, knowledge, frequencies, sounds, colors, existence, all matter . . . just simply everything is amalgamated within my light.

I am holding in my "body" the total balance of all things and all matters. My energy has the highest frequency there is. This frequency is radiating love, peace and balance constantly inward and outward. It pulsates very finely. It has such delicate wavelengths that it is very hard for you to notice.

Using your words we can also transform it to something like this:

My body is the light of All.
My energy is the heart of All.
My frequency is the pulse of All.

Now you may understand why people report that they are overwhelmed with love and peace, if they even get a tiny glimpse of me. Even if this glimpse was only a split second, they understand what is there to understand. All of a sudden they know what there is to know. Actually, you all know it all along, you only forget, because you get sidetracked from the concept you are living in. But this is a different story.

So, that is who I am, what I look like and whether I have a body or not. What's next?

Are you a "Supreme Being," or "God," or "Allah?"

My friend . . . I am not *"a"* anything. I am *"Is!"* No more no less!

People try to call me names. They try very hard to analyze me and figure out what I want, what I wish and what I expect. They try to fit me in their concept, in their idea of living. Some of you even try to use me for your own purpose and profit.

Ancient stories about me were modified many times. Then these stories were transferred into written words. Later you created books, and these already modified stories, were rewritten with lots of different ideas and explanations about me. People had different opinions about my expectations from you. You split up into groups and invented the illusion of a "right" or "wrong" way to please me. Finally, your arguments ended up in a big confusion.

As always, confusion leads mankind into overreacting.

Some of you even decided you have to fight over your opinions about me and believed this would solve your problems, for good. So these different groups marched into many wars with the impression that *I* would let the *right* party win.

Little did they know! I would never get involved in these kind of senseless activities!

All the more, none of them realized that they all acknowledge my existence in one form or another and that they fought over their absurd explanation about me.

Minor details!

Even if we take the hypothetical case and say I would involve myself with your fighting. Tell me . . . who shall I let win, if everybody has the basics right?

Well anyway, let's move on . . .

Mankind made me into a very complicated entity, with all kinds of human characteristics . . . and up to this point, your interpretation of me stayed the same.

Here, I'll give you an example:

You invented the *illusion* that I expect from you, that you do something for me. Sacrifice something on my account, or worship me in a certain way, otherwise I am not happy and I will punish you.

This idea is really funny!

Why do you think I would require that?
Is there any reason for that?

Do you really expect me to have an "Ego," which has to be satisfied and prove itself to somebody or something? Do you really assume that *I* have the **need** to prove **myself** to **myself**?

. . . That I occupy myself, telling me how **wonderful** and **great** I am, because today there were some more people around the world, who worshiped me the way I demanded.

 . . . That I sit somewhere **considering** different ways of punishment for the other ones?

Trust me . . . I do not concern myself with such foolishness!

The example above is only one and a very small one of your misconceptions about me. I do not expect or demand anything!

My dear . . . knowing that, we can go back to your question.
I am sure it is now easier for you to follow me:

I am none of the names mankind has given me!
I am way beyond that!

All these names are connected with earthly life concepts.
I am way beyond that!

All these names are attached to what you call "Religions."
I am beyond that!

All these names convert me into a Ruler, Dictator, Leader or a King.
I am none of these!

All these names turn me into a judge.
I am not a judge. . . ! I do not punish!

I repeat: I am very simple I am *"IS!"*

But you make things happen?

              Yes!

. . . and you hold everything together?

                Yes!

. . . and you don't want anything from us?

                  No!

But why are we here then?

Definitely not because I *want* something from you. My dear friend, let me inform you: . . . You are not living for *me!*

You are created from within me, . . . you are *my* creation, but you do not live *"for"* me. . . ! Why should you?

You live for you *. . . yourself. . . !* and that's it . . . *very simple!*

One of the biggest learning processes of mankind is acceptance. It is of some importance to accept what *is*. Some things are just too compact to be analyzed, categorized or put into a certain drawer. They just *are!*

. . . so, are we here to learn something?

No, not necessarily. But since you are here anyway, you might as well learn something.

Hey, cheer up my dear, there are many reasons why you are here. One of the reasons is to experience "being." Not very many of you seem to do so. Again, it is in the *simplicity* of the *matter!*

You always expect everything to be so complicated. Oh, now you think you have experienced "being" your whole life. You think you had heartbreaks, sadness, laughter, fun, worries and death in your nearest surrounding. You learned what you could in school, worked hard and earned money. You also went to parties, had fun, fell in love, married and had children. How much more "being" is there to experience?

Well, there is plenty!

See, most of what you enumerate here is *"living"* not *"being."* Living is an earthly life experience, which is a great adventure and another reason why you are here. . . ! But "Being" is a sacred experience with all kinds of wisdom and knowledge.

Let me unfold the difference between living and being.

Did you experience the growing of a flower, or the energy of a tree, or the love of your animal? Do not mix up experience with feeling now . . . ! There is a difference, you know . . . Yes, of course you know.

Again . . . Did you ever experience the great capacity of balance in your life, the notion of freedom or peace, the connection with reality and the universe? Or were you only occupied with life's necessities?

Did you ever swim in a pond and experience the water movement on your body, how it softly caresses your skin? Did you ever let the water run between your fingers and experience the consistency?

Or did you just jump into the pond and start your *"laps"* to get some exercise?

Did you ever experience "being" or are you only occupied with the experience "living?"

You are here to bring "being" into "earthly life!"

. . . That's a biggy . . . right?

You all are supreme **"Beings"** with the capacity to create, with the connection to the universes, with the knowing of all times, with the tight bonds with me, but you all are quite sidetracked.

There is this talk on earth in some religions about "paradise," or a "Garden of Eden," where everybody is in love, peace and awareness!

Who of you knows exactly where the Garden of Eden is?

Well, you don't, but I do . . . and I'll tell you: It is right in front of your noses, you are living in it, but you do not see it . . . and on top of that, you're trying to ruin it for thousands of years!

You do not believe me? **Well, well, well** . . . let me give you a hint:

If you could manage to understand "being" and "living" and combine both of them into total balance, you would be in **the** "Garden of Eden" of all times.

This would solve your problems immediately. There would be no suffering, no wars, no silly concepts anymore. These bring you nothing other than hardship and unhappiness. You would create respect for all things, all existence, known or unknown to you. In an instant you would understand, what there is to understand, you would cherish what there is to cherish and worship what there is to worship!

Then you would reveal the secrets of all life and all matters, on earth and in the universes. The "Paradise" or "Garden of Eden," you are praising so highly at the moment, would be all around you, and you created or re-created it.

It would not hurt to rethink your living concept, but that is your decision to make. I am not saying you **must** change it . . . ! You can all stay in your old concepts until the end of times. These concepts have proven to have a minimum risk for your life-span, and they have worked for many generations in the past, kind of . . . ! You will not live in the so-called paradise, but you will live!

. . . and it will work for you also, ***kind of***!

Well, enough of this . . . any other questions?

How powerful are you?

I can destroy universes with a blink of an eye! Well, don't make such a face . . .

What kind of comparison did you expect from me?

If you are so powerful, why don't you do something about our criminals, injustices or wars?

Hey . . . I am not a judge! I do not judge! Whatever happens, happens. For me, there is no good or bad. There is only *"IS!"*

. . . but isn't it wrong to kill other people?

So . . . but I do not run around and punish people who do not understand that. Please try to comprehend, I do not punish, I do not judge, I do not interfere. Earthly living is your creation! I created **life itself**, but not earthly living! You have the ability to create earthly life however you want and however it pleases you.

You do it . . . it's your "baby!"

. . . but, what about handicapped people?

Hey . . . another one you want to blame on me?

Well, first of all:
Who ever gave you the idea that nature has to be one-hundred percent perfect? Or, that under indescribable circumstances nature can not make any mistakes?

. . . and second:
Did you ever consider, that handicapped people suffer the most, because you treat them in certain way? Their suffering would be reduced, if your eyes did not tell them that you feel uncomfortable around them . . . if your actions would not show them that you only feel sorry for them.

If you could accept this as a fact of live and integrate it into your heart, they would still know they are different than most of the people in the world, but they would not suffer more because of their surroundings.

Yes, I created the world. But then I gave you the power to create a perfect world to live in.

Yes, I know you are trying very hard, but nobody told you it is going to be easy and that there wouldn't be setbacks . . . **right?**

Why don't you help us?

Oh, Dear . . . I help you all the time, but you do not listen! I would be very delighted if you would listen, once in a while. The moment you start listening is like a switch turning on the light.

All of a sudden everything will fall into place. But it is your choice. I am always here, you have to choose your way.

You create your life with your own choices. If you once made your choice, the whole universe is standing by to help you. Of course, this works for **any** direction, your decision is made!

If you make the choice to live a happy life, your vibration and frequencies travel all around you and also into the whole universe. They will meet the same vibration and frequencies out in space. Both of them will unite and your output will be enhanced by the strength of this alliance. It is working like an amplifying system and gives you more power to create whatever you want! In this case, to live a happy life. It will come quite easily for you, to achieve your goal. On the other hand, if you choose to live an unhappy life it will do the same . . . **sorry**! Now you're asking yourself the question: "Who on earth would choose an unhappy life?"

The answer is:
"Many, many of you . . . just look around you!"

See, I am helping you! I am helping you in many ways.

The only problem is, that I am not helping you the way you expect me to. You'd like me to take your hand and tell you what is right or wrong. You will promise me with all your heart, to follow any kind of instructions I will give you, like a very good little child follows his/her parent's rules. Of course, you expect a reward for this entirely good behavior of yours, something like the life you always wanted, the paradise you always dreamed of and the love you always desired. *Sorry, I can not do this!*

I am very well aware of the fact that your expectations do not come out of your own greed. It is how your concept has worked for hundreds of years and you got used to it. You make a bargain with everything and anything. "You give me this and because of this I give you that!" **Sorry, I cannot be a part of this system!**

In the minute you would have everything you asked for . . . well, at least . . . most of you, would start to find a way to ignore my instructions, or at least to find a nice way around them, with exceptional excuses, of course. Yes, you would!

Please look at it, without getting offended: You do not follow your own developed instructions, yet. Why should you follow mine? Yes, I know, most of your self-made instructions do not make any sense whatsoever! Mine would, for me, because I know! But what would happens if they do not make any sense to you? Trust me, you would wiggle yourself around them and hope that I wouldn't notice! Don't deny that . . . you are very "smart cookies!"

I also know exactly your capability . . . and it is enormous! Much more than you realize up to this point!

Yes . . . I know . . . I created you, remember? So, don't try to outsmart me. You should know by now that it doesn't work!

You go and make your own choices and decisions. You create your Garden of Eden . . . You can do it!

I will help you, but I will not make your decisions. It is not my nature to act as a prison officer and tell you what to do. I know that you have the capacity, the power and that you are mature enough to take your life in your hands. Just do it!

You know it all yourself, just listen and remember!

And for the ones that still need the proof you require in your society, turn to your scientists. They give you information about your capacity in your brain. Or look at your psychologists, who have more and more knowledge about the workings of your consciousness and your sub-consciousness. People who work in metaphysics reveal every day more and more about awareness and the "Beyond."

You have a wealth of information, accessible to nearly **everyone** as never before on earth. You invented certain teaching-systems for your children, which include training in reading and writing.

Your schooling also reveals to you, again, the process of thinking, which you conveniently forgot for a while.

In the **past**, only **some** people on earth had the pleasure to use these tools.

Up to now, you used them for the purpose to fit into your concept "society." This was like a training camp. Now you can use them for your own choices, for your own decisions and for your own creations.

Just try it. . . ! You have all the help you need around you. Make just a tiny little baby-step and you will see. . . ! You can make it . . . I know! Even if **you** don't believe in **yourself**, yet, *I believe in you!*

How did you do it?

What?

. . . Create the world and stuff?

. . . the world and stuff . . .

Okay . . . Creation is very easy! You do it all the time! You do it on a smaller scale than I, but you do it! Knowing you, you like to get formulas and calculations, right?

Some of you even picture in their mind, that I had to go to school and study in order to create!

No, no, my friends, I didn't have to do this, neither do you!

I could give you physical formulas and talk with you for days about physical laws, but it would not be of any use.

Not for you and not for me either.

I would lose you listening to my lecture, in about two minutes. Our physical and universal laws are very complex. Not all of them are understandable in the way you like to assemble them. It is anyway of no consequence for you at this point to know **why** they work a certain way, but it is important to know **how** it works.

If you first concede this, then the rest follows by itself!

I am before any matter. I make matter happen. How do I do this? Very simple. . . !
I do it with pure intention!

Here you find how it works:
It . . . breath . . . thought . . . intention . . . form (physical laws) . . . matter!

Hey, do not smile at me with doubt. . . ! It *"is"* what it *"is!"* and it *is* not very complicated!

If you understand or at least acknowledge this, it would help you tremendously.

Any kind of creation starts with a thought! Intention acts as the carrier to put this thought into manifestation. It is really very easy, and you do it all day long! In fact, you are so used to it that you do not even notice anymore that you are doing it.

It is like a perfume, or an after-shave you buy. In the beginning you spray it on and you smell it strong and very nicely. After a while you get so used to the smell that it fades away. Everybody else around you still notices it, but you don't recognize anymore if you are wearing it, or not.

One of the biggest differences between you and me is that I use my abilities with **full awareness** and you don't. You just do your thing and **flounder around and about** without any idea what you are doing.

Oh, yes . . . you use it alright. . . ! You as a single person use this power to create your personal life, your body, your direct surrounding. You as a mass of people use it, to create your earthly life.

You are not aware of what you are doing. You are not aware of it, because you use your powers without direct intention and direction. On top of it, most of you like to make somebody else responsible for your actions. I know, I know . . . you have been trained this way for many generations!

But now *"human beings"* entered a certain **adulthood** in the **cosmos** and the old excuses do not work anymore!

Everybody, *every single one of you*, knows enough today to understand all the powers given to you. Just use them and use them in full awareness, caution and responsibility.

You don't have to be a *rocket scientist* to figure it out!

Again, it is very easy!

It is actually lying on your doorstep . . . like a parcel you got in the mail, sent from a good old friend.

Think about it . . . what would you do, if you got mail like this?

You would open the door, reach down to the parcel, get quite excited and open it. Knowing that your friend would not send you something to your dislike, you unwrap your gifts and feel honored to have them received. After you've investigated your gifts, you would play with them and use them. All the more, you might like them so much, that you would carry them around with you or display them on a shelf in your living room. You would handle them very carefully and use them with a lot of caution, so that nothing would happen to them. If somebody else would like to play with them, you would make them aware, that you cherish these gifts and that they must handle them with circumspection.

You would do this, right?

Well, my dear friend you received a **huge parcel**, a long time ago. This parcel contained everything and anything you need and enjoy for all times, in all situations.

It was **me**, the oldest friend you have, who delivered the parcel to you and put it on your doorstep! It was **me**, who always will **love** you the most, who **selected** the gifts you found in this box! These gifts where **chosen** very carefully and especially for **you**, to **help** you, not to harm you!

The package was so full of presents, that most of you unwrapped and started to use them all at once. Since there were so many, you did not give yourself enough time to investigate them. Most of them have many features and functions.

Only very few of you took the time to examine their gifts truly. These few know more today than most of you.

These are the ones you seek to find and follow. These are the ones you tend to ask questions and for help. You cannot understand these because you are expecting a *"how to"* menu. These are the ones you like to have near you, sitting by their feet, hoping their wisdom and knowledge **rubs** off . . . and that at least some of it clings to you!

Well, you will have many disappointments if you try to find it somewhere else, than in your own gift-box. It does not rub off, there is no menu, and there is no blind following! **Stop** acting like children in kindergarden crying for Mommy and Daddy to help and tell. You are no child anymore.

Evolution transformed you into a universal "grown-up!"

If you, as your own person, should look at your gifts and tools again, you will be surprised at what you find!

If you, as a mass of people, look at all your gift-boxes, you will be even more surprised by what you find!

Use your gifts with caution . . . they are very **powerful**. If you use them right, they will work *for* you not **against** you . . . you will see!

Use them with care and responsibility! Not only in respect for yourself, but also for consideration of others, your surrounding, your planet, your universe!

Keep in mind that there are many ways to reach your goals and to achieve what you want to achieve, whatever it is!

There is a lot of help around you. You just have to look!

. . . and remember always: "I am forever here to help you!"

If you do not notice my help at once, look deeper, closer or from a different angle. As I said before, I do not work in the ways you are used to.

On your journey, please keep in mind that some of you will find the answers they need in their heart, others in the nature around you, some in the universal teachings, others in existing religions, others through meditation, some sitting at the feet of a guru!

Some will find the answers while they are gardening, or while they are jogging, or while they enjoy sitting in the sunshine!

There are many ways to find the answer. The way is not important, the outcome is!

Remember it is **your** creation, **your** life and **your** planet, you're dealing with!

So, my friend, I think with this knowledge, you can find your way easily. I answered many questions for you and it is time for you to go to work, on the matters, I pointed out to you **. . . *if you choose to do it!***

Wait, wait . . . I have still so many questions!

Well, why don't you try out your tools and gifts and find the answers by yourself? That will be so much more fun for you.

Don't get in panic, it will be easy, trust me! Here I start to repeat myself already a couple of times. I am not fond of that. It's wasted energy!

We could go on talking for weeks, have many more examples and there would be always the same explanations.

It would be so boring for you and senseless for me . . . But once again: **"You can reach me all the time!"**

But when can I talk with you again?

As I said, you can reach me at any time, but I normally do not use your known words and language. Words written or spoken are very confusing and limited.

You invented so many different languages on your planet, that even you have difficulties to translate one to another.

Words are incomplete and the foundation for all misunderstandings!

I do not like to be misinterpreted, because of your words . . . therefore, I do not like to use them! Since I saw many of you being unhappy and lost for a long time, I made an exception today. I **choose** to adopt your words to get in **contact** with you.

My language is universal!

It contains frequencies, wavelengths, signs, notions, feelings, sound, energy, light, geometry etc. **Everything** and **anything** can understand my language. My language is not limited to "human beings." Of course, you can understand it too, you only have to listen!

Okay . . . but how can I reach you?

. . . do I have to be enlightened to do so?

What are you talking about? Maybe you should start to read this book again from the beginning!

No . . . seriously . . . what you understand as "Enlightenment" is a certain state of mind. You call people "enlightened," who you think know more than others about the secrets from the "Beyond."

The truth is that they already remembered what seems to be forgotten for a long time. It is not a new science, as some of you presume. It is as old as me and you.

These people you call "enlightened" started a while ago, thinking about the same things, we are talking about here, now. They already found out, that everybody can put themselves into this state of "Enlightenment."

By now they also understand the **simplicity** behind it!

Once they established themselves into this state of mind, you feel a strong devotion around them.

Then you start calling them "enlightened."

If you like to do this, you can do it and you are very welcome, but you don't need it to reach me!

Wise people told you, in the past, many times. And in some of your books it is written. You know what? They got it—**kind** of right!

But now, *I* will tell you. **Please listen!**

I am all around you, I am within you, I am in the air you breath, in the food you eat, in the water you drink, in the animal you pet, in the stone you touch, in the soil you cultivate, in the earth you live on, in the wind you feel, in the sun that warms you, in the rain that gives you water, in the sound you hear, in the notion you sense, in the vibes you receive and in the cracker you nibble on!

So, see . . . I am never far away from you!

If you would like to reach me, just get quiet . . . and I will be there!

With "getting quiet" I do not mean that you can not speak . . . no, no, no!

Just sit down, and take a minute out of your life and get quiet!
Let your body and mind relax.
Let your thoughts drift away.

If you still have thoughts, label them thoughts and release them into space.

Get quiet!
Get present in the moment!
Get quiet!
Sense the space between the moments!

In this moment and just for right now . . .
there is nothing to do . . .
nowhere to go . . .
nothing you want . . .
and nothing missing!

Be quiet!
Get present in the space between the moment . . .

. . . and now you talk to me and ask your questions.

I will give you the answers in the form of notions, pictures and images. Seldom, we'll talk through your known words. I know you do not like this too much, but look at it this way:

You will learn once again the universal language.

This will come in handy for you, for all kinds of purposes in the future. With the understanding of the universal language comes a tremendous amount of **"Knowing"** back to you.

"Knowing" that you knew before and all along, but just forgot.

. . . and I:

I will be there**, for you and with you, **for all times.

. . . and you:

You will remember who you are!

Who are you anyway?

My friend, let me introduce yourself to you . . .

You
You are
You are "You"
You are "You" from where everything rises.
You are the emptiness before thought.
You are the essence from the essence.
You are the beginning of the beginning.
You are the creator of the creation.
You are the silence before matter.
You are everything and nothing.
You are the simplicity in itself.
You are "You"
You are
You

You are that for what you have no words.

You are "You" and as by now, only a few of you got a glimpse of you.

That's who you are!

Dear friend, please know:

> **I am you . . .**
>   **and you are me** . . .
>   ***and we are "IS!"***